GW01164581

Radical
Forgiveness

Radical Forgiveness
A Handbook for Spiritual Growth
by Blake Steele
Copyright © 2003 Scandinavia Publishing House
Drejervej 11-21, DK 2400 Copenhagen NV, Denmark
Tel.: (45) 35310330   Fax: (45) 35310334   E-Mail: jvo@scanpublishing.dk
Text copyright © 2003 Blake Steele
Photo copyright © 2003 Blake Steele
Design by Ben Alex

Printed in Singapore
ISBN 87 7247 263 4

All rights reserved. No part of this book may be reproduced or utilized in any form or by any means, electronic or mechanical, including photocopying, recording, or by any information storage and retrieval system, without permission in writing from the publisher.

Spiritual Vision Series
by Blake Steele

A God to Desire
Being Loved
Radical Forgiveness
Creative Compassion

SPIRITUAL VISION SERIES

RADICAL FORGIVENESS

A HANDBOOK FOR SPIRITUAL GROWTH

WORDS AND PHOTOGRAPHY
BY BLAKE STEELE

scandinavia

4

As I worked on this manuscript I realized how extensive a subject forgiveness is. There is God's forgiveness of the world and of us as individuals. Then our forgiveness of ourselves, letting go of self-judgments, some of which we have held since we were children; also letting go of judgments we project on others; our forgiveness of those who have truly hurt us; asking forgiveness of those we have hurt; our forgiveness of the world; and even our forgiveness of God.

This is a little book. Therefore I can only briefly touch upon these important subjects with the hope that you might be inspired to embrace the gift of forgiveness in all its dimensions and thus become the freest, most beautiful person you can be for the glory of God.

BLAKE STEELE

FORGIVE AND YOU WILL BE FORGIVEN. LUKE 6:37

Forgiveness is ultimately about spiritual freedom. When we understand the New Testament meaning of the words translated forgiveness it is clear that the two topics are inseparable.

The Greek word Apoluo is used in the verse above. It means to *free fully, let go,* or *release*. So Jesus is literally saying, *Set free and you will be set free.*

The word Aphiemi is used in many other places and means to *send away, yield up, let go* and *let be.*

7

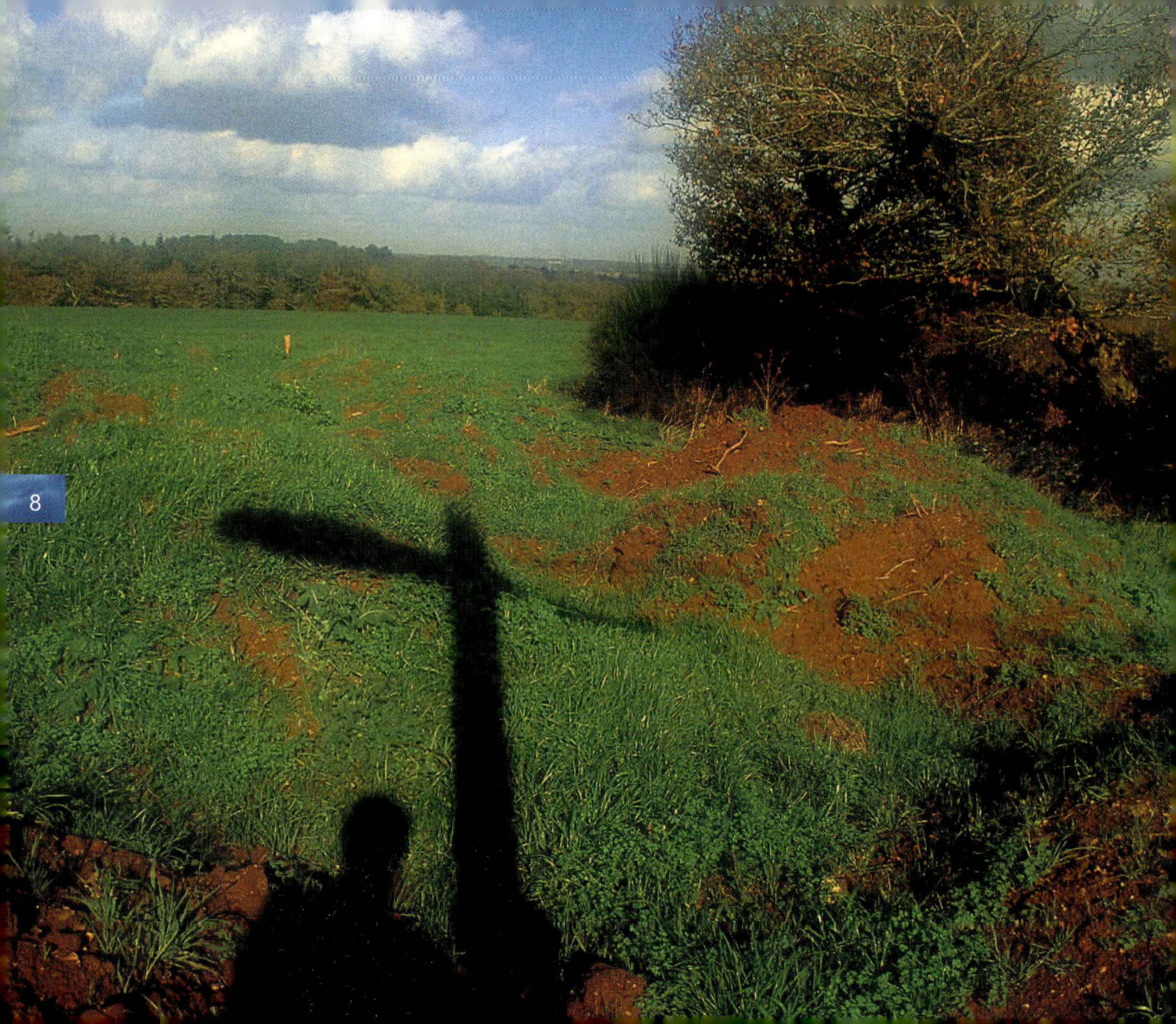

8

It was for freedom that
Christ set us free... Gal 5:1

Radical forgiveness is based on God's complete forgiveness and acceptance of us in Christ. It is developing a heart that freely forgives your self, others, the world, and even God so that you can live more openly and naturally in the grace and wonder of Love. It is a commitment to release and send away whatever binds and constricts your soul in order to experience the fullness of life in the freedom of Christ.

Because God radically forgives us, we can forgive others and ourselves all the way to joyous liberty and peace. Does this sound too good to be true? Just open your heart. Let God surprise you.

THE LORD GIVES GRACE
AND GLORY... PSALM 84:11

11

12

WHERE THE SPIRIT OF THE LORD IS,
THERE IS FREEDOM. II Cor 3:17

God is free. There is no fear in God; nothing oppressive; nothing bound; nothing shamed. Life creatively dances in God. Love is the free-flowing good will of His Being. It brings pleasure to God when we open to receive His Love and learn what it is to be truly free—for in God Love is pure freedom.

The Living God is beautiful beyond all imagining,
oceans of Love and rivers of Light;
motionless, silent, eternal, serene—
and bubbling up, bounding
in a pleasure-filled fountain
of free-flowing Spirit—
the God who is waiting for us to desire
Love to transform us in pure joy forever.

14

15

> GOD WAS IN CHRIST RECONCILING THE WORLD TO HIMSELF, NOT COUNTING THEIR TRESPASSES AGAINST THEM... II COR 5:19

God was in Christ, reuniting the world to Himself—for this is the meaning of the word reconciliation. The Holy God who once required sacrifice to atone for sin gave His Son to be the sacrifice and through him descended into the depth of human depravity and despair. In that act of complete union with us, compassion is revealed as the only true justice. Our trespasses are not counted against us for all legal demands are nullified, all debts have been paid in full. Now there is only grace and forgiveness as a transformative way.

God has embraced the world to His heart and His arms are wide open to us.

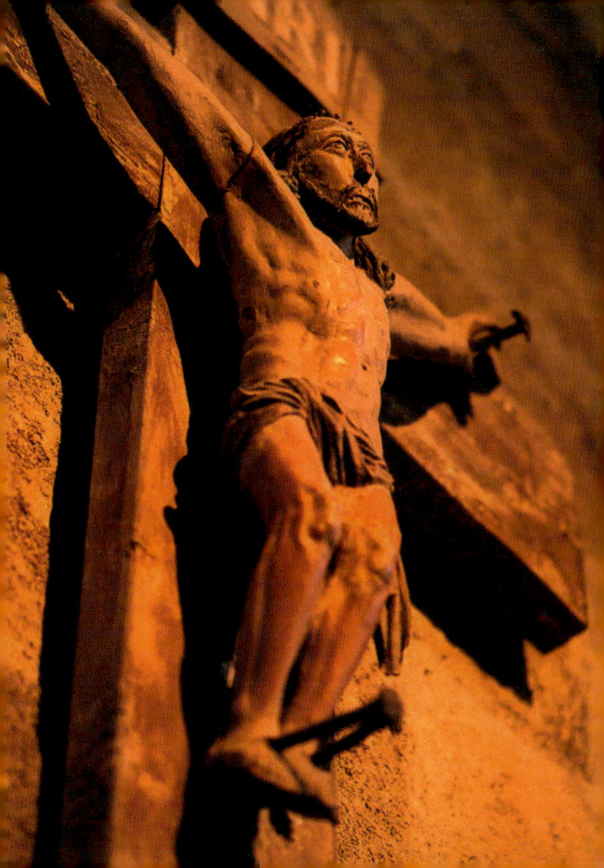

18

Now this expression,
"He ascended," what does it
mean except that He also had
first descended into the lower
parts of the earth? Eph 4:9

From the bloody cross of shame,
from blinding, electric pain,
from dirty metal, torn flesh and tears
His prayer arose,
"Father forgive them,
for they know not what they do."
Through our confusion and ignorant dark,
into our worst fears and howl of grief
he descends, down into the agony of our despair.
From hell itself His cry ascends,
"Look, Father! I am in them..."
It is from there that He arose.

> HE WHO DESCENDED IS HIMSELF ALSO HE WHO ASCENDED FAR ABOVE ALL THE HEAVENS, THAT HE MIGHT FILL ALL THINGS. EPH 4:10

Christ knows how hard it is to be human. He is one of us. He is in us. He knows each of us has been wounded in the most innocent and vulnerable depths of our heart and in that pain of grief fallen headlong into the dark of alienation. And He knows there is only one thing that can heal our wound and bring us back to Him, and that is the power of unconditional Love.

> TAKE COURAGE, CHILD, YOUR SINS ARE FORGIVEN. MATTHEW 9:2

All that matters to God is welcoming us home to His heart. Forgiveness is a wide open door into the feast of His Love. Take courage. We never have to beg for forgiveness. He loves to set us free from all that holds us back.

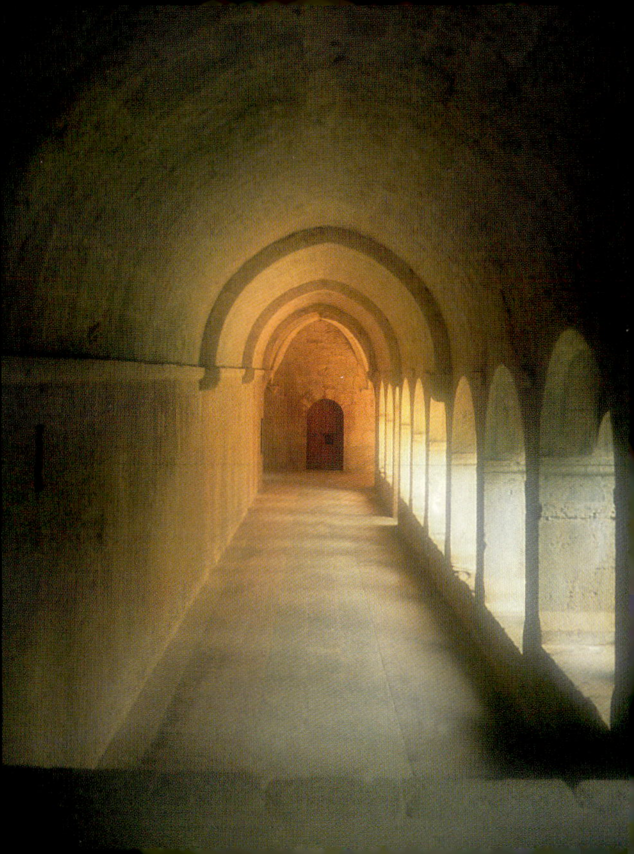

22

> BUT WHILE HE WAS STILL A LONG WAY OFF, HIS FATHER SAW HIM, AND FELT COMPASSION, AND RAN AND EMBRACED HIM, AND KISSED HIM AGAIN AND AGAIN. LUKE 15:20

Jesus' parable of the prodigal son reveals the compassionate heart of God. The son who had been reckless and degenerate ends up in a desperate situation and decides to return home. While he is still a long way off, his father runs to him and kisses him again and again. "Bring the robes," the old man cries. "Put rings on his fingers. Prepare a great feast. My child has come home!"

This beautiful story pictures the unconditional acceptance and warm welcoming of God's heart. There is not the slightest hint of judgment or displeasure that the son had publicly shamed him. All the wayward son did was accept his father's love and the music began.

> Now the older son...became angry,
> and was not willing to go in; and his
> father came out and began entreating
> him. Luke 15:25-32

Meanwhile, his older brother was angry and would not enter the feast. He felt the father's compassion was unjust. He demanded fairness according to rules of righteousness. He was the one who had stayed at home, faithfully serving his father, never neglecting his commands, yet when his brother who had wasted his father's wealth with drunkenness and wild carousing comes home, the fatted calf is killed.

The father did not judge the older son either, but tenderly called him, My child, imploring him to enter the celebration of his compassion. But he would not go in. His own judgments excluded him.

25

26

27

> DO NOT JUDGE LEST YOU BE JUDGED YOURSELVES. FOR IN THE WAY YOU JUDGE, YOU WILL BE JUDGED; AND BY YOUR STANDARD OF MEASURE, IT SHALL BE MEASURED TO YOU. LUKE 6:37

Jesus says do not judge, for we are judged by our own judgments. It is our self-created judgments that bind and blind us. All our lives our hearts have been formed by judgments. Every judgment is a personal interpretation of our experience, a deep inner belief that becomes the source of countless thoughts, emotions and attitudes that rise within our hearts. This pattern of inner judgments and beliefs colors our perception of life.

All judgments that block us from fully welcoming God's compassionate Love into every room in our hearts must be undone if we are to know His freedom.

A person who cannot forgive is like a gazelle with one leg or a swan with no feet.

29

30

*I want to write to your most deep and tender heart
that wants, above all things, to be free,
to grow, to open to the light of God's Love
without a trace of anger, without a dark spot of shame.
Forgive yourself for the Lord's sake.
Give up your judgments, your old agreement
that you would inflict punishment on yourself
because of your fear of going astray.
There is not one judgment that is right
unless it leads to Love's freedom.*

> FOR NEITHER IS CIRCUMCISION ANYTHING, NOR
> UNCIRCUMCISION, BUT A NEW CREATION. GAL 6:15

All that matters to God is a new creation, not judging or regulating the old one. Our judgments and anxious efforts to fix our selves only get in His way for it is Christ that is the new creation of compassion and spiritual beauty.

> CHRIST IN YOU, THE HOPE OF GLORY. COL 1:27

And Christ is in us. He is the mirror in which our true life is revealed. For Christ is the fountain of Creation, the miraculous Light of true being. From Him pours forth the pure creative power of Life to recreate our hearts. From Him pours forth our deepest instincts for Love to heal and liberate our world.

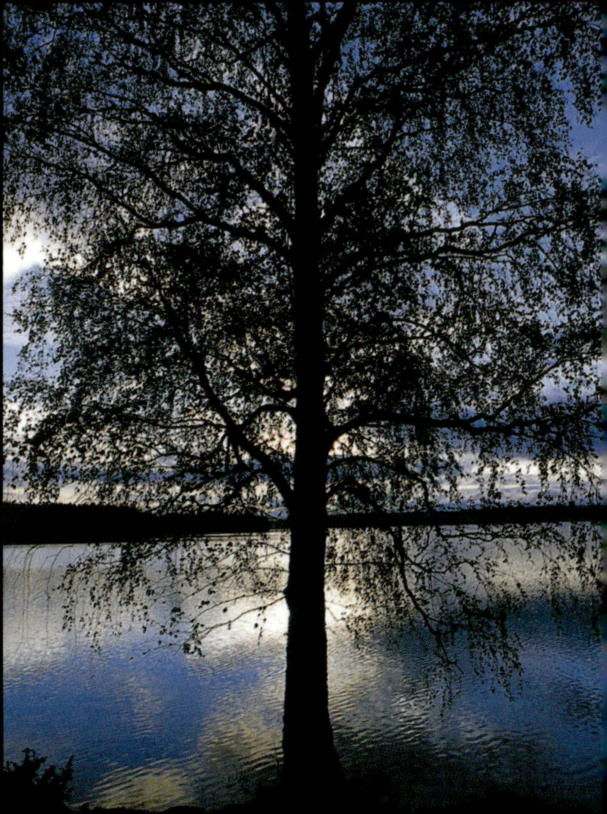

34

*Healing is having one intent:
to heal, to open, to let Love
flow through unhindered—
to be free.
This is one intent
expressed in different ways.
Healing is opening to God.*

> ON THAT DAY YOU WILL REALIZE THAT I AM IN MY
> FATHER AND YOU ARE IN ME AND I AM IN YOU. JOHN 14:20

To become whole, our outer man must wholly yield to the Life of Christ in our innermost being. To accept this grace our soul must soften, for the gift is tender, and flows to us through our most vulnerable heart.

> HE GATHERS THE LAMBS IN HIS ARMS AND
> CARRIES THEM CLOSE TO HIS HEART... Is 40:11

Only unconditional Love can soften us. Only forgiveness can unblock us. Only as we allow God's complete acceptance of us, just as we are, with all our wounds and unresolved conflicts, can our deep heart open and let Christ embrace our entire being into His warm, loving heart.

37

38

She was beautiful with light:
her eyes, her smile seemed to shine,
her hands shined.
The radiance was unmistakable.
I asked her, "How, why?"
She said, "I am loved without limits...
and God, the glorious maid, vacuums my soul
while Christ, the beautiful washerwoman,
cleanses my linens, and fresh Spirit pours."
I asked, "Is this infectious?"
She whispered, "Yes."

Self-Forgiveness

> Forgive as the Lord forgave you. Col 3:13

We forgive to unblock and open ourselves completely to our deepest, truest being. Ultimately, we will forgive others only as freely as we allow His forgiveness of us.

Radical forgiveness is complete self-acceptance: a compassionate welcoming of all that is within us into God's heart—especially what we are ashamed of, have avoided, rejected, and judged.

Welcome home anger. Welcome home bitterness. Welcome home anxiety. Welcome home shame. Welcome home my most painful experiences. Welcome home my whole being to the open arms of Love.

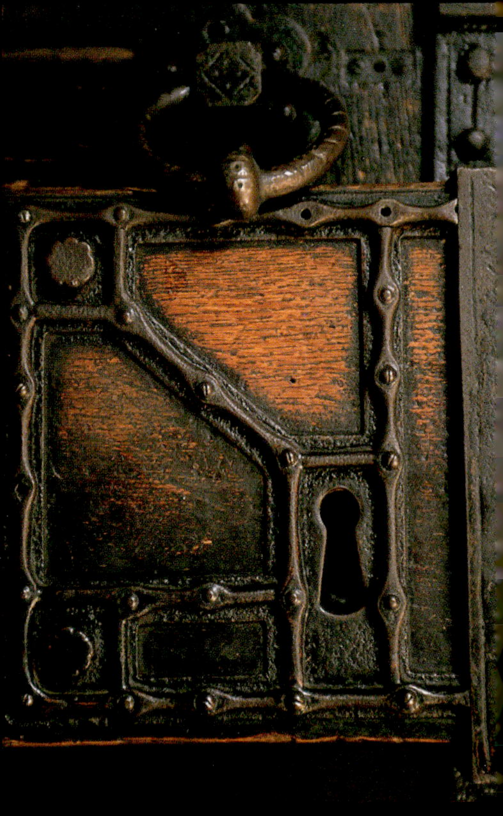

42

43

> GOD HAS POURED OUT HIS LOVE INTO OUR HEARTS
> BY THE HOLY SPIRIT WHOM HE HAS GIVEN US. ROM 5:5

Just make a commitment to forgive and welcome everything within you home to Him and you will find yourself as a host in the feast of His Love. You will center yourself in Christ's grace and the Holy Spirit will pour God's Love out of your innermost being. This welcoming naturally shifts you from self to Christ. It frees God to free you. It is complete self-acceptance that honors His ability to transform all things by Love.

> FOR NOT EVEN THE FATHER JUDGES ANY ONE... JOHN 5:22

Meeting and welcoming all that is within you is not the same as approving of everything. On the contrary, you are neither approving nor disapproving. You are no longer acting as judge. You are giving up judgment altogether. You are admitting you are not wise enough to do God's work. Now, the One who does not judge is your only judge. He is the One who saves.

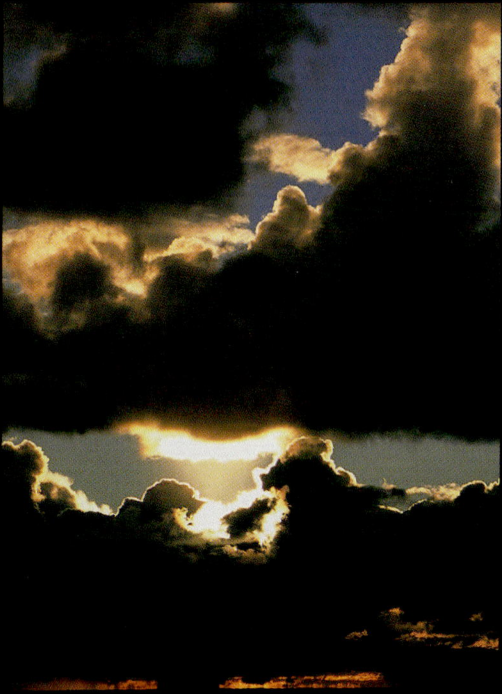

46

WE LOVE BECAUSE HE FIRST LOVED US. I JOHN 4:19

But if we don't judge ourselves, won't we freely live out our patterns of loveless actions? It might seem that way to our mind at first, but in reality it is just the opposite. Why do we do loveless actions? Isn't it because of the lack of Love in our hearts? Love comes from God, not self. If self is judging self it is still self. We remain stuck in self, and that is our problem. What is needed is to harmonize our heart and mind with His—to let His Life come through. Therefore, surrender is the way. It is God's unconditional Love meeting everything within us that transforms us.

What is needed is a new center:
an open heart, a tender yielding to being forgiven,
to being loved without limits.
Out of this center flows His Love for the world.

*Why do we need to hold onto our judgments,
our guilt, our self-censure and bitter blame?
Is it because we are afraid that if there is no punishment
we will run amuck, go wild, be abandoned
in our severed sense of self?
Come home, cherished child.
It is only Love that melts us into Love.
It is only grace that makes our hearts gracious.
It is only God's compassionate freedom
that sets us utterly free.*

49

50

BUT WE HAVE THE MIND OF CHRIST. I COR 2:16

As self-judgment is undone the light of Christ shines brighter in our hearts and Love flows more spontaneously through our being. What replaces self-judgment is clear seeing. Rather than confining and repressing us, this clarity of discernment reveals a deeper level of wisdom that leads us in the way of Love's freedom.

BUT THE WISDOM FROM ABOVE IS
FIRST PURE AND PEACEFUL, GENTLE
AND WILLING TO YIELD... JAMES 3:17

This wisdom is peaceful and full of mercy, without a hint of hypocrisy, for it allows us to be open and honest regarding all we really are. Being born of gentle compassion it welcomes our entire human condition in the unconditional acceptance that allows change to happen freely.

> THE LORD SETS THE PRISONERS FREE. THE LORD
> OPENS THE EYES OF THE BLIND... Ps 146:7,8

Unconditional welcoming and self-forgiveness comes from God, through us. It is not merely a concept we hold in our mind. It is not an emotion we create. You cannot locate the source of it in yourself. We can only let go with child-like trust and surrender to accept it. It is what remains when all self-judgment is undone. It is the liberating action of Christ. It is God's saving grace allowed.

> GOD BE GRACIOUS TO US AND BLESS US, AND
> CAUSE HIS FACE TO SHINE UPON US. Ps 67:1

As we become warmly undressed of self-judgments we discover that underneath them is the bright face of Love we have always longed to know. Our heart, full of Love's welcoming becomes God's kingdom, and our truest home.

53

54

TEST ALL THINGS; HOLD FAST TO THAT WHICH IS GOOD. I Thess 5:21

But don't just believe me. Test everything. Only this way will you know for yourself the power of His radical forgiveness to free you. Next time a negative feeling about your self comes up, welcome it fully into God's warm embrace. Forgive yourself and let God's Love kiss that negative feeling again and again. Let God warp arms of Love around old wounds and new. See what it is like to bring your entire self home. Discover how such grace will make you open and humble, noble and real. Come home to His Love.

Give the go–a–head to God.
Pour resistance into a cauldron of the sun.
Listen to every alienated voice
and bring the prodigals home to Love.
Then the heart will remain open without effort
and the flowing Wisdom will flood.

56

Practice His welcoming of you for a day; then make it two. Once this welcoming of your whole self into His Love gets a foothold in your heart, nothing can stop it. The fountain of grace is open and flowing. With self-judgment dethroned, everything within you is free to come home, for in Christ all is eternally forgiven. And God is free to come home to you.

For the Love of Christ, forgive yourself quickly and completely. Embrace your entire life. Be the one who welcomes your resistance of His Love into His Love. He will wash it all away.

Wash in the river of God,
for it is clear, clean, innocent Life.
Hold nothing back. Let it spill all over you.
Take a shower. Take a bath.
This is His free gift...
Open up. Dive in.

When You Miss the Point

When you act from your wounded nature, just be completely honest. Because God loves you limitlessly, you can be open and completely real. No one expects a cow to fly. Why do we expect our alienated sense of self to express the freedom of His Love? It is the nature of our alienated self to miss the mark, the meaning, the point of Life.

Apart from Him we are a closed door,
a shivering gazelle hiding in a bush,
clinched fists grasping for wind,
busyness with too little meaning,

59

60

Confess your sins to one another and pray for one another, so that you may be healed. James 5:16

Just see your old, wounded nature for what it is. Honestly admit its futility. Though self-judging doesn't work, complete honesty does. Be transparent. It is a wonderful relief to let your genuine hypocrisy be revealed. Talk to God: shift yourself right back into God's warm embrace as the beloved one who welcomes your whole soul home to His Love.

Every time your old nature comes up, it is show time! It is time for transformative welcoming; time to practice radical forgiveness; time to grow freer. Realize what a gift life has given you. What an opportunity you have to grow in Love!

(See appendix for additional help.)

Forgiving Others

> And whenever you stand praying forgive, if you have anything against anyone; so that your Father also who is in heaven may forgive you your transgressions. Mark 11:25

In forgiving others it is important to realize that first and foremost you are not releasing others from the wrong they have done, but releasing yourself from the effects of the wrong done. It is about turning your pain into compassion. It is about your freedom.

We must be committed to freedom. Yield to Christ's passion for you to be free. Be committed to allowing Him to melt your resistance to His will completely with His Love. It is this committed choice that releases the power of God to bless you without limits.

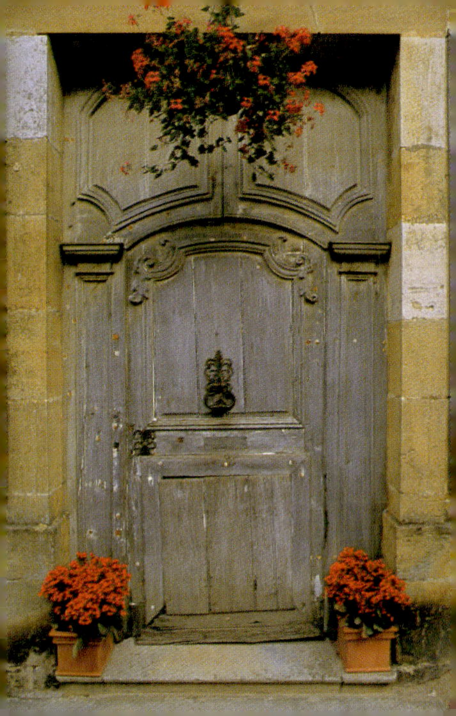

64

65

*I protest all self-imposed limitations
to the delicious beauty of God's Love.
Let my song crumble every demand for retribution.
To live life with a heart of stone
is a crime against the gentle light of wild stars.
When the deep, tender-heart that was wrapped in pain
and smothered with fear is set free,
love's song dances through our blood without words,
without music, without aching need.*

67

68

When You Have Been Wounded

When someone has cruelly abused you, the emotional pain can go very deep. This is especially true of childhood abuse. With this kind of pain we usually cannot let it go until the grief that is connected with it has been fully heard and affirmed. Life-altering abuse robs us of innocence and wounds us with the grief of loss. As Jesus fearlessly descended into human pain for us, so to heal, we also must open our pain and let it be heard.

Recognize your grief. Welcome it. Embrace it. Feel it fully. Let the tears fall. There may be tremendous anger. It is ok. Be true to what is in you. Be utterly real. God's Love for you will not fail. Would you rather live your life holding the pain deep within, a secret poison in your body and soul? Forgiveness must come through a complete embracing of the wound itself. Jesus forgave from the cross. Break through fear; meet your pain. Only then will your wounded heart be willing to forgive.

> GOD CAUSES ALL THINGS TO WORK TOGETHER
> FOR GOOD TO THOSE WHO LOVE GOD AND ARE
> CALLED ACCORDING TO HIS PURPOSE. ROM 8:28

To refuse to forgive those who have hurt us is to side with retribution instead of redemption. We make our heart a courtroom and take the seat of both the judge and the victim. By insisting on punishment we lock up ourselves.

The truth is that all we have experienced is an important part of our eternal journey. It happened. It is real. It is part of you, and no matter how hurt you have been, God's intent is to turn every wound into spiritual strength and beauty. As long as you feel like a victim it is almost impossible to completely forgive. Once you realize that by fully embracing your experience you are actually recovering your life and freeing God to turn all you suffered into wisdom and compassion—it is a brand new world! You step out of the victim mode and enter your truest purpose. With that shift, you can let go of your role as judge as well as victim and be free.

71

> BUT I SAY TO YOU WHO HEAR,
> LOVE YOUR ENEMIES... LUKE 6:27

Yield to your higher purpose. Give up the resentment you think you have the right to hold and offer compassionate love to the person you think does not deserve it. This is the path to your own freedom.

Forgiveness breaks the poisonous cycle of hurt, grief, resentment, hatred and revenge. Every abuser has been abused. They have caused you pain because someone else hurt them. To forgive your abuser is to melt away the animosity in your heart. What is left is not an enemy, but a person who needs forgiveness and love just as much as you.

73

74

If we could see the secret life of those we would like to see punished, we would find so much grief and suffering that we would feel like criminals wishing anything more upon them. And if we could journey with God to the deepest core of this person's pain, we would find a blind child, lonely, afraid, weeping, crying out for Love, for the light of life. And our whole instinct for Love would impel us to take this child into our arms and love them completely.

When You Have Hurt Others

When your wounds have caused you to hurt someone else, it is important to ask for their forgiveness. In this way you initiate an opportunity to heal.

> And why do you look at the speck that is in your brother's eye, but do not notice the log that is in your own eye? Luke 6:41

The confidence that comes from fully embracing God's forgiveness of you will drop the mental defenses that blind you from seeing how you have wounded them. Your radical self-acceptance enables you to clearly see what you have avoided in your life and to move through any fear of shame or rejection. Acknowledging the truth and asking for forgiveness is always a liberating act, no matter how the other person responds.

77

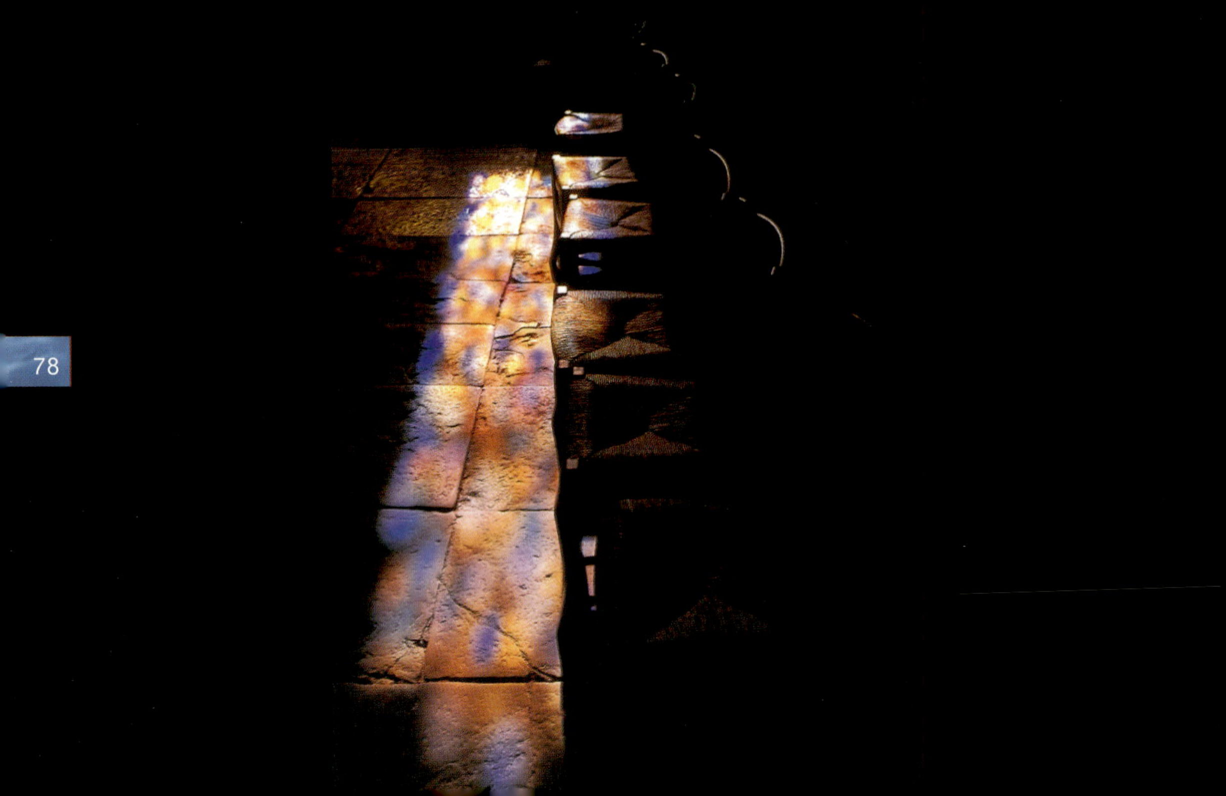

Because they hurt me, I have hurt you.
And in wounding you my grief deepened.
I did not want to rain poison arrows
down into your dreams.
Bitterness had blinded me:
but now a Love beyond all telling;
now the grace that turns all things around;
now pain itself becomes the seed of this pearl—
compassion.

> ...FIRST BE RECONCILED TO YOUR BROTHER, AND
> THEN COME AND PRESENT YOUR OFFERING. Mat 5:24

Be reconciled if possible. But if this is not possible, let it go. We cannot liberate others. That is God's job. It is such a relief to let go of the burden of trying to make others change.

When the other person is still deeply entrenched in an abusive way of being, it is our open honesty and firm commitment to be free that protects us. The more you are free from self-judgment in your own heart the more clearly you can see the games of accusation and blame other people play to protect themselves. If you judge them at all you are trapped in the blame game. Instead, just observe what is happening and step out of it. Let go. Let be. Forgive. Once you are no longer abusing yourself you realize you really are free to walk away from abusive situations.

81

82

Truly I say to you, whatever you shall
bind on earth shall be bound in heaven,
and whatever you loose on earth shall
be loosed in heaven. Matt 18:18

In truth, there is such creative freedom in Christ that like Him we can hold all people beautiful in our hearts. Though people may be bitter, angry, or depressed in themselves, they can be beautiful and full of Love within us.

Once we realize the difference between the person "out there" and their image and influence within us, we can let go of all anxious effort to change the outer person and work very freely with the inner one. Through forgiveness, we can let go of all the negative emotions and attitudes we have towards them.
This transformation in our heart has a greater power and influence than we may imagine, for what we loose on earth shall be loosed in heaven.

84

Do good to those who hate you,
bless those who curse you, pray for
those who mistreat you. Luke 6:27,28

By offering total acceptance to the outer person, just as they are, and then blessing them abundantly in your heart, God is free to work healing miracles in His own time and way.

Pray for them. Wish God's greatest blessings of happiness upon them. Transform the hurtful things they express to you by blessing them lavishly within your soul. This is the creative, redemptive power of faith working through Love.

Imagine them blessed. Take time to daydream of streams of living water, clear as crystal, shinning and shimmering, spilling all over them, washing all pain, all negative attitudes and emotions away. Picture their face joyous, loving, and utterly beautiful in Christ.

> IF YOU FORGIVE THE SINS OF ANY, THEIR SINS HAVE BEEN FORGIVEN THEM; IF YOU RETAIN THE SINS OF ANY, THEY HAVE BEEN RETAINED. JOHN 20:23

Through this simple, child-like exercise of Love, your heart will grow free and beautiful and something wondrous will be loosed in heaven.

Grace, grace, glorious grace: the fountain of His Spirit flowing to draw them, woo them, win them, touching their most tender, and vulnerable hearts as only God can do.

Changing people is God's job. Leave it in His hands. Your job is to be free in His Love. You can hold all people beautiful in your heart. You can bless everyone and your whole heart will be blessed. In this way, you become a living prayer of intercession for their freedom. And the Love that is freely working within your mind and heart will spontaneously overflow in your words and actions.

87

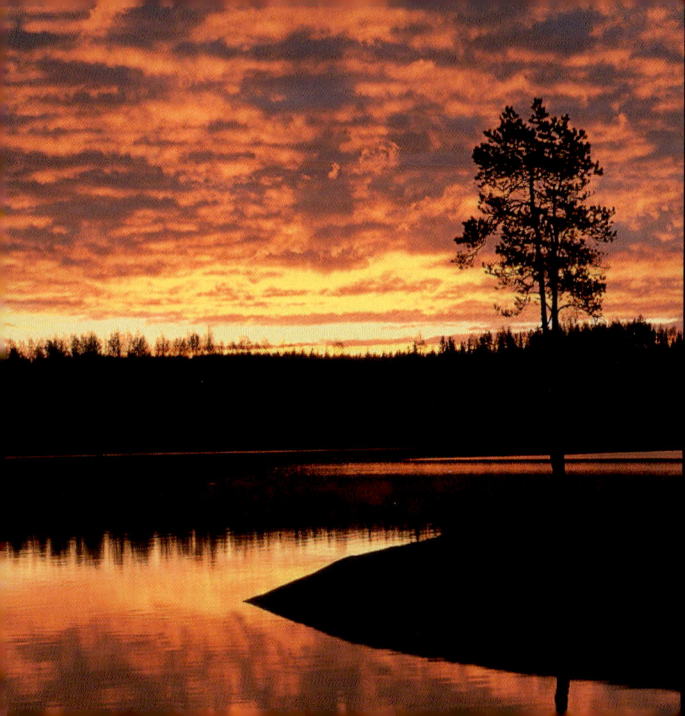

FORGIVING THE WORLD

FOR GOD SO LOVED THE WORLD... JOHN 3:16

God has forgiven the world. Have you? God loves the world so much He gifted it with sun, moon and stars, an astonishing variety of food, birds and animals, sunrises and sunsets, billions of people, His own Son as Savior, and children of His Love everywhere. Do you love and appreciate the world? Or are you trapped in critical judgments?

It is profoundly true that we see life through who we are. Therefore, the world mirrors our hearts to us. It holds all possibilities. To the fearful, it is a dangerous place. To the creative, it is bursting with potential. To the judgmental it is totally flawed. To those who live in Love and awe, it is full of God.

Let Go And Let Be

Forgiveness is acceptance. Accept the world, just as it is. God knows exactly what He is doing. This world is the perfect place to grow a compassionate and forgiving heart. Therefore, give up trying to change the world to make you happy. You must change to make you happy, and when you do, all the world you touch will be blessed.

Don't interrupt the sweet presence...
keep on opening, keep on forgiving.
Don't interrupt the pure joy...
keep on trusting, keep on playing.
Don't interrupt the action of Love...
keep on drinking, keep on spilling the cup.

91

92

93

FORGIVING GOD

Forgiveness cannot become complete without forgiving God. I know this may sound strange to some people at first, but our intuition tells us that a Creator of infinite intelligence and wisdom must be the one ultimately responsible for everything. And so, for everything beyond our control and life's most painful experiences, something deep within us cannot help but hold God responsible.

Perhaps you need to forgive God for putting you here in this world; or for the family you were born into; or for your looks; or for your body's natural capabilities; or your mental abilities. Have you forgiven God for pain and disease so you can embrace life fully? Have you forgiven God for unexplainable tragedies? Can you forgive God for untimely deaths, for the loss of loved ones, and for the terrible shock of death itself?

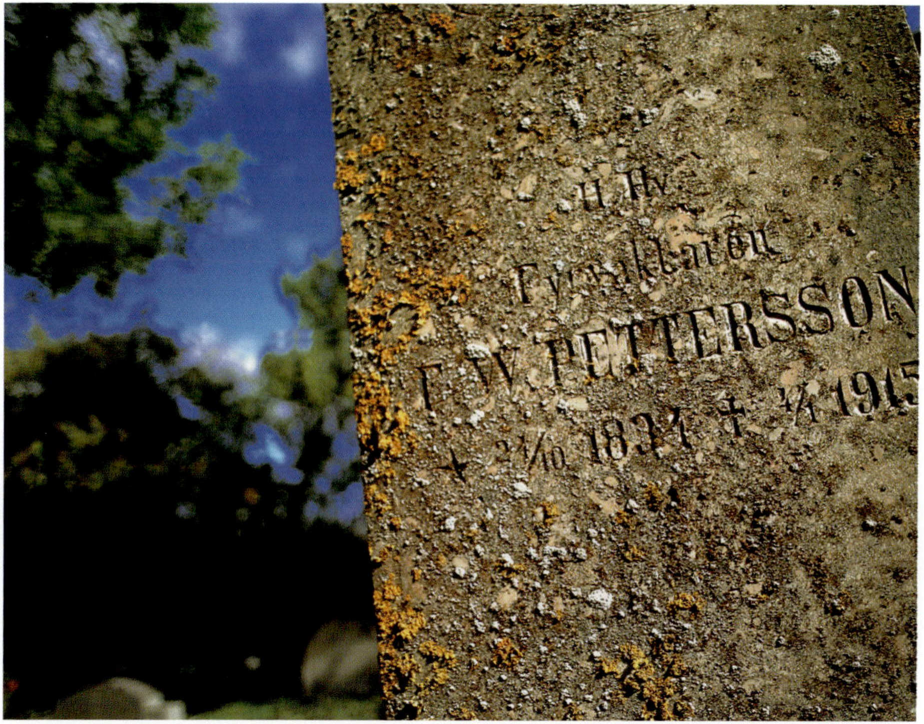
Fyrvaktaren
F W PETTERSSON

Does our need to forgive God imply that He is at fault? No, it is just the opposite. It is to discover that we can fully face and embrace life as it is with complete honesty. Our forgiveness of God is an act of transcending our pain and grief in order to trust once again in His Love; it is to acknowledge the reality of human suffering and all our unanswered questions and at the same time humbly bow before His infinite wisdom and let life as it is mold us into the compassionate beings we are here to become.

Because God forgives us completely He can see us creatively, as beautiful beings, new creations in Christ. And so, because we completely forgive Him, we can continually set God free in our hearts to be our God, the infinite Love and beauty who is the source and ultimate meaning of our lives.

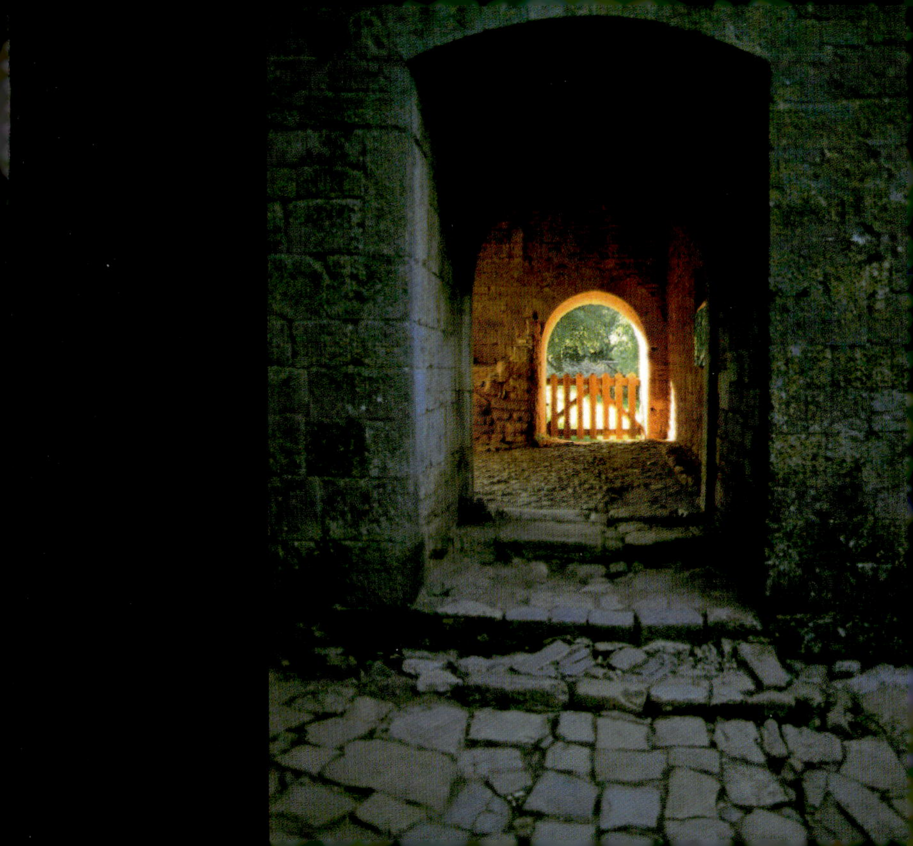

98

*Let go of all that resists Love
and red balloons are set free
in an ocean of sky.
The whole river of Life
moves through your opening being
as it is meant to.
Without envy or bitterness
or anger or fear, what is left?
A mystery of beauty
beyond the power of words to tell.*

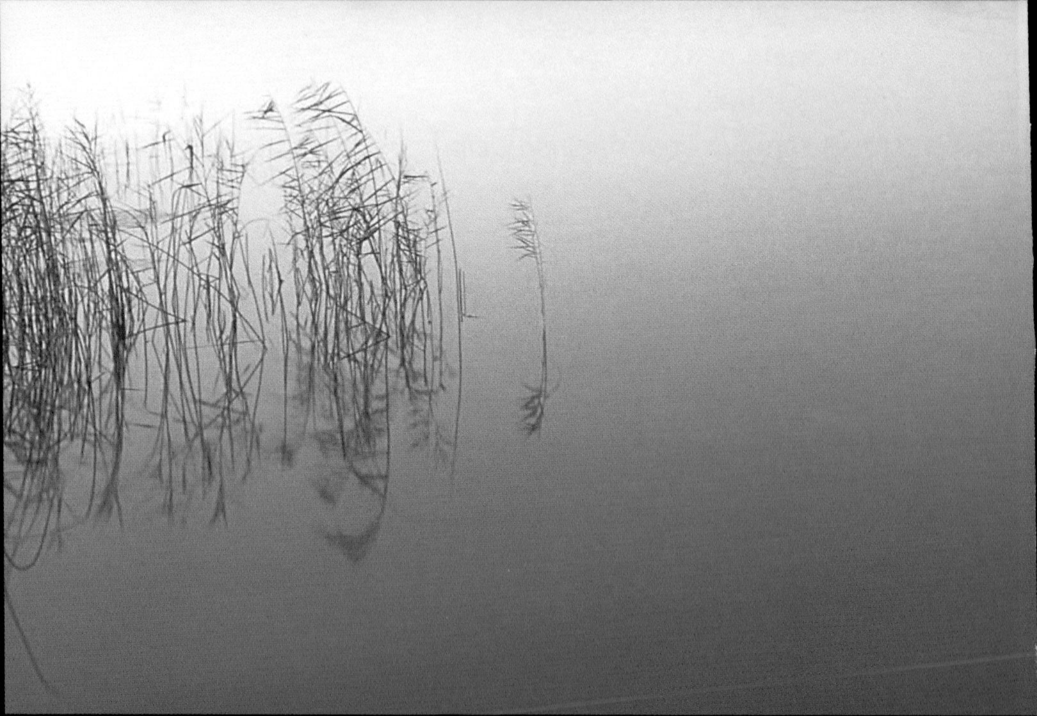

101

APPENDIX

Turning Things Around

Here is an additional way to undo stubborn, deeply rooted negative judgments that cause habitual thoughts, attitudes and actions.

> MAKE FRIENDS QUICKLY WITH YOUR ADVERSARY...
> UNLESS HE DELIVER YOU TO THE JUDGE AND
> YOU BE THROWN INTO PRISON. MATT 5:25

As first, welcome and make friends with each negative emotion and old judgment that arises in you. Feel it fully. Observe it with compassion. Don't put your identity in it and you won't attach to it. In this way you will be dead to sin and alive to God. You are not insecurity. You are not cynical. You are not worthlessness. You are hidden with Christ in God, luminous, noble, loved without limits, already safely at home.

BUT I SAY TO YOU, DO NOT RESIST
HIM WHO IS EVIL... MATT 5:39

This principle of non-resistance is very important for our inner life. Don't resist anything within you. Resisting resistance increases resistance. Feeling frustrated about anger increases anger. Feeling critical about criticalness feeds criticalness. Being anxious about anxiety intensifies it. And saying I won't do it again, doesn't work.

Negative emotions and judgments lock each other in place in our hearts and become our prison. Shame feeds the fear that feeds the defensiveness that frustrates you and makes you feel ashamed, etc. This is why it is essential to not identify with any of it but to break completely out of the pattern. Only by neither being nor resisting nor denying the existence of the old self are you free to let God redirect and transform it.

Repent, the kingdom of heaven has come near. Matt 4:17

Listen to what arises in you. Lovingly ask it questions without fear. Let it feel what it feels and reveal what it has to say. Once you have fully heard a negative self-judgment then you can turn it around and undo it by asking it a few simple questions that replace the false belief at its root with the truth. Turning things around is Christ's way. Repentance means just this: to turn around, or change your mind. Whatever binds us is not rooted in God's truth; therefore, truth will undo it. Each inner judgment you question and turn around is confounded, weakened, and in time completely undone.

Radical forgiveness is replacing a faulty belief in our heart with a new one that is in harmony with the Love of Christ. It is a restructuring of our nerves, our brains, our bodily cells. It is true transformation.

BE TRANSFORMED BY THE RENEWING
OF YOUR MIND... ROM 12:2

4 Questions To Turn Old Judgments Around*

This little exercise is very effective. It will work most powerfully if you write it rather than just thinking it through. Putting it on paper focuses it with great clarity in your heart.

1. After the self-judgment has fully expressed what it needs to say, ask it, *Is this actually true?* Listen for the answer.

Usually the first answer that comes up is that it feels true. Of course it does, because it seems so familiar. Therefore, it is *essential* to ask the question again, *Can you be completely sure that this is absolutely true?* and listen. (Write it down.)

*Thanks to Byron Katie and her work.

2. Then ask yourself, *In the light of God's Love, what is true?* And allow all the saving grace of God's passion for you to be whole and beautiful and free in Christ speak through your thoughts. Listen. Bask in it. Bathe in it. (Write it down.) This is your true life—the Love that saves.

3. Now ask, *How has identifying with this negative judgment made me feel?* Listen fully. *And how has it made me act?* (Write it down.)

4. Then ask, *How does believing the voice of God's Love make me feel?* Feel this fully. *And how would I act?* (Write it all down.)

107

Now make a clear choice what you will now believe. If your choice is for God's grace then reverse the old judgment, turn it completely around. Whatever it said about you and your situation, say the exact opposite. (Write it down.)

Think your situation through again with grace, with complete forgiveness, with welcoming, with the Love that alone makes all things new. Thinking it through again allows the Light of Life to renew your mind. New perspective comes and with it, everything shifts.

Each time our heart shifts, life is never again the same. Jesus spoke again and again of the importance of what we believed in our hearts. Radical forgiveness reprograms the heart to believe in goodness beyond understanding, in Love beyond all conception, in beauty beyond imagining. It moves our identity from separateness and limitation to union with Christ and centers us in God's wholly creative way of seeing us. Radical forgiveness is Christ's way for His light to grow brighter and us to grow free.

110

*All judgments we make are presumptuous.
Let them come. Let them make their case.
One little question and they fall apart.
"Is this really true?" One more question
and they are blown away like a gnat in an oceanic wind,
"Does this judgment lead to God's freedom?"*

Blake Steele is one of God's vagabonds on earth, traveling to do creative work and share God's abundant love through personal encounters and workshops. A versatile artist, he has written over 2,000 poems, a novel, children's stories, is a lyricist for choral pieces and a photographer. In this book series, he shares his vision, wisdom and awe for God through photography and poetic writing.

www.beingloved.net

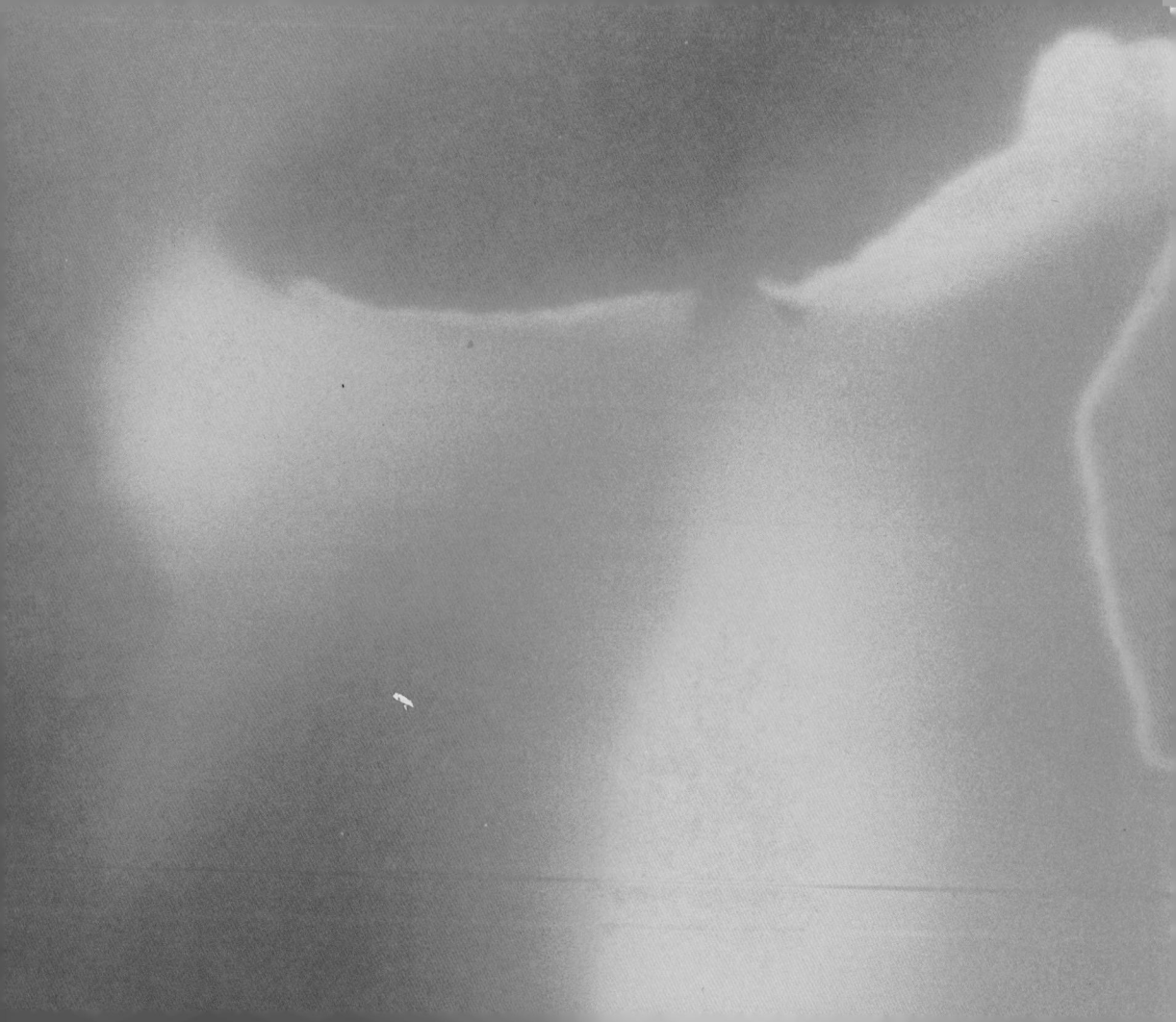